50 INSTAGRAM AND FACEBOOK ADS: A PRACTICAL GUIDE 2024

HOW TO CREATE PROFITABLE SOCIAL MEDIA ADS FOR WELLNESS AND HEALTH BUSINESSES

A.V. SOUTELO

DEDICATION

To all the dreamers turned doers, the small business owners, and the relentless entrepreneurs:

This book is dedicated to you—the visionaries seeking to leave a mark in the digital marketplace. May these pages serve as your guide to mastering Instagram and Facebook ads, unlocking the full potential of your brand, and achieving the success you've worked tirelessly to attain. Here's to increased sales, flourishing businesses, and the transformative power of a well-crafted ad. May your passion be matched by your growing success.

CONTENTS

1 New Client Offer   Pg 11

2 Benefits of Detox Massage   Pg 12

3 Gift a Session   Pg 13

4 Client Before and After   Pg 14

5 Ocean Breeze Bliss   Pg 15

6 Starry Night Serenity   Pg 16

7 Forest Retreat   Pg 17

8 Limited Time offer   Pg 18

9 Why Choose Us   Pg 19

10 Meet our Therapists   Pg 20

11 Cient's Review   Pg 21

12 Self-Care Tips   Pg 22

13 Referral Program   Pg 23

14 Full Moon Special   Pg 24

15 Celebrating Women's Day   Pg 25

16 Couple's Retreat   Pg 26

17 Early Bird Special   Pg 27

18 Birthday Special   Pg 28

19 Group Booking Bonus   Pg 29

20 Autumn Serenity   Pg 30

21 Post-Workout Wind Down   Pg 31

22 Sleep Sanctuary Session   Pg 32

23 Digital Detox Day   Pg 33

24 Anti-Aging Alchemy   Pg 34

25 Golden Hour Glow   Pg 35

26 Tropical Tranquility   Pg 36

27 Migraine Mitigation Magic   Pg 37

28 Breathe Easy Eucalyptus   Pg 38

29 Serene Stress Melt   Pg 39

30 Luminous Skin League   Pg 40

31 Detoxify your Life   Pg 41

32 5 Signs you Need a Spa Day   Pg 42

33 Journey to Relaxation   Pg 43

34 Beat the Work Stress   Pg 44

35 Hydration Heaven   Pg 45

36 Back Pain Be Bone   Pg 46

37 Age Gracefully   Pg 47

38 The Anti-Stress Toolkit   Pg 48

39 Glowing Maternity Moments   Pg 49

40 Detox Dynamics   Pg 50

41 Quick Stress-Buster Massage Techniques   Pg 51

42 Hydration Heaven Water-Based Spa Treatments   Pg 52

43 Aromatic Bliss – Essential Oil Collection   Pg 53

44 The Ultimate Relaxation Package   Pg 54

45 Detox Delight   Pg 55

46 Deep Sleep Inducing Massage Techniques   Pg 56

47 Herbal Steam Therapy – Detoxify your Body   Pg 57

48 Revitalize with our Signature Facials   Pg 58

49 Ultimate Hydration Therapy   Pg 59

50 Garden Serenity   Pg 60

INTRODUCTION

In the ever-evolving landscape of digital marketing, social media platforms like Instagram and Facebook have emerged as powerful tools for wellness and health businesses. These platforms offer an unparalleled opportunity to reach a broad audience, engage with potential clients, and grow your brand. However, creating ads that capture attention, convey your message, and drive action can be challenging.

This book, "50 Instagram and Facebook Ads: A Practical Guide 2024", is crafted to address this challenge. Within these pages, you will find a collection of 50 meticulously designed ad examples, each tailored to resonate with the wellness and health sector's unique audience. These examples are more than just templates; they are a source of inspiration and a blueprint for success.

Here's how to make the most of this guide:

1. **Understand the Strategy**: Each ad in this book comes with detailed descriptions of its elements, including the sentiment it evokes, the format it uses, and the specific category it targets. Understanding these aspects will help you grasp the strategy behind each ad.
2. **Customize with Your Brand**: Use these examples as a starting point. Adapt the language, imagery, and overall concept to fit your brand's voice and aesthetic. Remember, consistency with your brand identity is key to recognition and trust.
3. **Engage with Creativity**: Don't be afraid to experiment. The ads in this book are meant to ignite your creativity. Mix and match elements from different examples and come up with something uniquely yours.
4. **Focus on Your Audience**: Every ad should be created with your target audience in mind. Consider their preferences, pain points, and what motivates them. This guide provides diverse

examples that cater to various segments of the wellness and health market.

5. **Measure and Optimize**: Finally, the effectiveness of an ad is proven by its performance. Use the insights from your ad campaigns to understand what works best for your audience. Adapt and refine your strategy based on real data.

As you delve into this guide, you will discover a wealth of knowledge and ideas that can transform your social media advertising approach. Each ad is a piece of a larger puzzle in building a successful digital presence. Embrace these insights, unleash your creativity, and watch your wellness and health business flourish on Instagram and Facebook.

Let's embark on this journey to mastering social media advertising together!

AD 1: NEW CLIENT OFFER

Parameter	Description
Sentiment:	Excitement
Post Format:	Image with Text Overlay
Category:	Promotion
Language:	Short caption
Theme:	New Client Offer
Idea:	Special discount for new clients.
PHOTO:	Relaxing spa ambiance.
TEXT OVERLAY:	"First-time clients: Get 30% off!"
CAPTION:	"New -to your business? Experience our services at a discounted rate. Book now! " #Your hashtags
CTA:	"Click the link in bio to book your session!"

AD 2: BENEFITS OF DETOX MASSAGE

Parameter	Description
Sentiment:	Informative
Post Format:	Carousel
Category:	Education
Language:	Short captions on each slide
Theme:	Benefits
Idea:	Highlight the top benefits of detox massage.
CONTENT:	Slide 1 = "Boosts Immunity", Slide 2 = "Improves Blood Circulation", Slide 3 = "Reduces Stress", Slide 4 = "Eliminates Toxins", Slide 5 = "Enhances Skin Glow"
CAPTION:	"Discover the multifaceted benefits of our detox massage. Swipe to learn more! " #Your hashtags
CTA:	"Ready to reap the benefits? Book your session today!"

AD 3: GIFT A SESSION

Parameter	Description
Sentiment:	Generosity
Post Format:	Image with Text Overlay
Category:	Promotion
Language:	Short caption
Theme:	Gifting
Idea:	Promote gifting a massage session to a loved one.
PHOTO:	Gift box with spa essentials.
TEXT OVERLAY:	"Gift a Relaxing Session!"
CAPTION:	"The perfect gift for your loved ones – a rejuvenating detox massage" #Your hashtags
CTA:	"Purchase a gift voucher now!"

AD 4: CLIENT BEFORE & AFTER

Parameter	Description
Sentiment:	Transformation
Post Format:	Side-by-side Image
Category:	Testimonial
Language:	Short caption
Theme:	Before & After
Idea:	Show a client's transformation after a detox massage.
PHOTO:	Left = Client before, Right = Client after.
TEXT OVERLAY:	"See the Difference!"
CAPTION:	"Real results from real clients. Experience the transformation yourself " #Your hashtags
CTA:	"Book your transformative session today!"

AD 5: OCEAN BREEZE BLISS

Parameter	Description
Sentiment:	Refreshment
Post Format:	Reel
Category:	Themed Promotion
Language:	Short caption
Theme:	Ocean
Idea:	A calming video of ocean waves paired with spa sounds.
VIDEO:	Ocean waves with overlay of spa treatment visuals.
TEXT OVERLAY:	"Experience the Ocean Breeze at Detox by Rebecca"
CAPTION:	"Let the ocean waves guide you to relaxation" #Your hashtags
CTA:	"Dive into relaxation! Book now!"

AD 6: STARRY NIGHT SERENITY

Parameter	Description
Sentiment:	Tranquility
Post Format:	Story with Poll
Category:	Night-time Promotion
Language:	Short caption
Theme:	Stars
Idea:	Promote a nighttime spa package under the stars.
STORY:	Starlit sky with spa setup.
TEXT OVERLAY:	"Would you spa under the stars? Yes/No"
CAPTION:	"Starry nights and spa delights. What's your pick? #Your hashtags
CTA:	"Wish upon a star! Book your night spa now!"

AD 7: FOREST RETREAT

Parameter	Description
Sentiment:	Rejuvenation
Post Format:	Reel
Category:	Nature Retreat
Language:	Short caption
Theme:	Forest
Idea:	A longer video showcasing a forest-themed spa retreat.
VIDEO:	Forest ambiance with spa treatments.
TEXT OVERLAY:	"Forest Retreat with Detox by Rebecca"
CAPTION:	"Nature's embrace and spa grace. Dive into our forest retreat" #Your hashtags
CTA:	"Embrace nature's touch! Book your forest retreat now!"

AD 8: LIMITED TIME OFFER

Parameter	Description
Sentiment:	Urgency
Post Format:	Image with Text Overlay
Category:	Promotion
Language:	Short caption
Theme:	Limited Offer
Idea:	A special discount available for a limited time.
PHOTO:	Sand hourglass or clock.
TEXT OVERLAY:	"48-Hour Flash Sale! 25% Off!"
CAPTION:	"Time is ticking! Grab this exclusive offer before it's gone" #Your hashtags
CTA:	"Hurry! Click the link to book now!"

AD 9: WHY CHOOSE US?

Parameter	Description
Sentiment:	Trust
Post Format:	Carousel
Category:	Branding
Language:	Short captions on each slide
Theme:	USP (Unique Selling Proposition)
Idea:	Highlight the unique features of your service.
CONTENT:	Slide 1 = "Experienced Therapists", Slide 2 = "Organic Oils", Slide 3 = "Customized Sessions", Slide 4 = "Hygienic Environment", Slide 5 = "Affordable Rates"
CAPTION:	"Why choose YOUR BUSINESS? Swipe to find out!" #Your hashtags
CTA:	"Experience the best. Book now!"

AD 10: MEET OUR THERAPISTS

Parameter	Description
Sentiment:	Introduction
Post Format:	Carousel
Category:	Team
Language:	Short captions on each slide
Theme:	Introduction
Idea:	Introduce the therapists and their expertise.
CONTENT:	Slide 1 = "Meet Anna - Expert in Swedish Massage", Slide 2 = "Meet John - Deep Tissue Specialist", Slide 3 = "Meet Emily - Aromatherapy Guru"
CAPTION:	"Our therapists are our strength. Swipe to meet our team!" #Your hashtags
CTA:	"Book a session with our experts today!"

AD 11: CLIENT'S REVIEW

Parameter	Description
Sentiment:	Appreciation
Post Format:	Image with Text Overlay
Category:	Testimonial
Language:	Short caption
Theme:	Positive Review
Idea:	Share a glowing review from a client.
PHOTO:	Relaxed client post-session.
TEXT OVERLAY:	"Best massage ever! - Jane"
CAPTION:	"Hearing from our satisfied clients makes our day! #Your hashtags
CTA:	"Join our list of happy clients. Book today!"

AD 12: SELF-CARE TIPS

Parameter	Description
Sentiment:	Informative
Post Format:	Carousel
Category:	Tips
Language:	Short captions on each slide
Theme:	Self-Care
Idea:	Share self-care tips for relaxation at home.
CONTENT:	Slide 1 = "Epsom Salt Bath", Slide 2 = "Lavender Essential Oil", Slide 3 = "Deep Breathing Exercises", Slide 4 = "Herbal Tea Before Bed"
CAPTION:	"Self-care is essential. Swipe for some relaxation tip" #Your hashtags
CTA:	"For a deeper relaxation, book a session with us!"

AD 13: REFERRAL PROGRAM

Parameter	Description
Sentiment:	Encouragement
Post Format:	Image with Text Overlay
Category:	Promotion
Language:	Short caption
Theme:	Referral
Idea:	Promote a referral program for clients.
PHOTO:	Two friends at the spa.
TEXT OVERLAY:	"Refer a Friend, Get 15% Off!"
CAPTION:	"Share the relaxation with friends and get rewarded!" #Your hashtags
CTA:	"Know someone who'd love our services? Refer them now!"

AD 14: FULL MOON SPECIAL

Parameter	Description
Sentiment:	Mystical
Post Format:	Image with Text Overlay
Category:	Promotion
Language:	Short caption
Theme:	Full Moon
Idea:	A special offer during the full moon.
PHOTO:	Night spa setup with a full moon in the background.
TEXT OVERLAY:	"Full Moon Special: 10% Off!"
CAPTION:	"Harness the energy of the full moon with a detox massage" #Your hashtags
CTA:	"Book your moonlit relaxation session now!"

AD 15: CELEBRATING WOMEN'S DAY

Parameter	Description
Sentiment:	Empowerment
Post Format:	Image with Text Overlay
Category:	Celebration
Language:	Short caption
Theme:	Women's Day
Idea:	A special offer for Women's Day.
PHOTO:	Group of diverse women relaxing at the spa.
TEXT OVERLAY:	"Women's Day Special: 20% Off for All Ladies!"
CAPTION:	"Celebrating the strength and grace of every woman. Happy Women's Day! " #Your hashtags
CTA:	"Ladies, pamper yourself today. Book now!"

AD 16: COUPLE'S RETREAT

Parameter	Description
Sentiment:	Romance
Post Format:	Image with Text Overlay
Category:	Promotion
Language:	Short caption
Theme:	Couples
Idea:	Promote a special package for couples.
PHOTO:	A couple enjoying a spa session together.
TEXT OVERLAY:	"Couple's Retreat: 15% Off!"
CAPTION:	"Reconnect and relax with your loved one. Experience our couple's special" #Your hashtags
CTA:	"Book a romantic session for two now!"

AD 17: EARLY BIRD SPECIAL

Parameter	Description
Sentiment:	Motivation
Post Format:	Image with Text Overlay
Category:	Promotion
Language:	Short caption
Theme:	Early Booking
Idea:	Offer a discount for bookings made in advance.
PHOTO:	Sunrise or morning spa setup.
TEXT OVERLAY:	"Early Bird Gets 20% Off!"
CAPTION:	"Plan ahead and save! Book your session 2 weeks in advance and enjoy a discount" #Your hashtags
CTA:	"Secure your spot and save today!"

AD 18: BIRTHDAY SPECIAL

Parameter	Description
Sentiment:	Celebration
Post Format:	Image with Text Overlay
Category:	Promotion
Language:	Short caption
Theme:	Birthday
Idea:	Offer a birthday discount.
PHOTO:	Spa setup with birthday decorations.
TEXT OVERLAY:	"Birthday Bliss: 25% Off!"
CAPTION:	"Celebrate your special day with relaxation. Enjoy our birthday treat for you!" #Your hashtags
CTA:	"Is it your birthday month? Book now and celebrate with us!"

AD 19: GROUP BOOKING BONUS

Parameter	Description
Sentiment:	Community
Post Format:	Image with Text Overlay
Category:	Promotion
Language:	Short caption
Theme:	Group Booking
Idea:	Offer a discount for group bookings.
PHOTO:	Group of friends enjoying spa treatments.
TEXT OVERLAY:	"Group Booking: Get 15% Off!"
CAPTION:	"Gather your friends and make it a spa day! Special discounts for group bookings" #Your hashtags
CTA:	"The more, the merrier! Book for your group today!"

AD 20: AUTUMN SERENITY

Parameter	Description
Sentiment:	Calm
Post Format:	Image with Text Overlay
Category:	Seasonal Promotion
Language:	Short caption
Theme:	Autumn
Idea:	Promote a fall-themed spa package.
PHOTO:	Autumn leaves and spa setup.
TEXT OVERLAY:	"Fall Special: 10% Off!"
CAPTION:	"Embrace the cozy vibes of fall with our special treatments" #Your hashtags
CTA:	"Fall for relaxation! Secure your spot today!"

AD 21: POST-WORKOUT WIND DOWN

Parameter	Description
Title	Post-Workout Wind Down
Sentiment	Relief
Post Format	Reel
Category	Pain Relief
Language	Empathetic and Encouraging
Theme	Sports Recovery
Idea	Presenting spa treatments that help with muscle recovery after workouts.
TEXT OVERLAY	"Soothe Your Muscles"
CAPTION	"Tired muscles? Our post-workout treatments are the perfect remedy" #Your hashtags
CTA	"Ease your strain, book a recovery session now."

AD 22: SLEEP SANCTUARY SESSION

Parameter	Description
Title	Sleep Sanctuary Session
Sentiment	Restful
Post Format	Reel
Category	Sleep Improvement
Language	Soft and Soothing
Theme	Insomnia Solutions
Idea	Showcasing treatments that promote better sleep, like aromatherapy.
TEXT OVERLAY	"Dream with Us"
CAPTION	"Struggle with sleep? Our relaxation therapies invite a night of peaceful dreams" #Your hashtags
CTA	"Discover your sleep sanctuary. Book a relaxation therapy today."

AD 23: DIGITAL DETOX DAY

Parameter	Description
Title	Digital Detox Day
Sentiment	Refreshing
Post Format	Reel
Category	Stress Relief
Language	Clear and Invigorating
Theme	Tech Stress Solutions
Idea	Highlighting a spa package designed to reduce digital stress.
TEXT OVERLAY	"Unplug with Us"
CAPTION	"Overwhelmed by screens? Our Digital Detox Day will recharge your spirit" #Your hashtags
CTA	"Turn off to tune in. Reserve your tech-free tranquility now."

AD 24: ANTI-AGING ALCHEMY

Parameter	Description
Title	Anti-Aging Alchemy
Sentiment	Hopeful
Post Format	Reel
Category	Age-Defying
Language	Positive and Assuring
Theme	Youthful Glow
Idea	Showcasing anti-aging treatments and client testimonials.
TEXT OVERLAY	"Turn Back Time"
CAPTION	"Seeking a youthful glow? Our anti-aging treatments work like magic" #Your hashtags
CTA	"Rejuvenate your skin. Book your anti-aging treatment today."

AD 25: GOLDEN HOUR GLOW

Parameter	Description
Sentiment:	Radiance
Post Format:	Carousel Images
Category:	Themed Promotion
Language:	Short caption
Theme:	Sunset
Idea:	Showcase a series of treatments best enjoyed during sunset.
PHOTO:	Series of treatments under sunset lighting.
TEXT OVERLAY:	"Golden Hour Specials: Swipe to see more!"
CAPTION:	"Experience the magic of golden hour with our treatments" #Your hashtags
CTA:	"Glow with us! Book your sunset session now!"

AD 26: TROPICAL TRANQUILITY

Parameter	Description
Sentiment:	Relaxation
Post Format:	Image with Text Overlay
Category:	Themed Promotion
Language:	Short caption
Theme:	Tropical
Idea:	Promote a tropical-themed spa package.
PHOTO:	Tropical fruits and spa setup.
TEXT OVERLAY:	"Tropical Bliss: 10% Off!"
CAPTION:	"Dive into a tropical paradise with our spa treatments" #Your hashtags
CTA:	"Escape to paradise! Book your session today!"

AD 27: MIGRAINE MITIGATION MAGIC

Parameter	Description
Title	Migraine Mitigation Magic
Sentiment	Soothing
Post Format	Reel
Category	Wellness
Language	Compassionate and Professional
Theme	Headache Relief
Idea	Offering a look at specific massages and therapies for headache relief.
TEXT OVERLAY	"Headache Relief Here"
CAPTION	"Migraines can be a pause button on life. Our treatments offer relief and relaxation" #Your hashtags
CTA	"Lift the weight off your head. Schedule a migraine relief session."

AD 28: BREATHE EASY EUCALYPTUS

Parameter	Description
Title	Breathe Easy Eucalyptus
Sentiment	Revitalizing
Post Format	Reel
Category	Respiratory Wellness
Language	Enlightening and Refreshing
Theme	Holistic Healing
Idea	Showcasing eucalyptus steam treatments for respiratory benefits.
TEXT OVERLAY	"Clear Airways, Clear Mind"
CAPTION	"Need a breath of fresh air? Our eucalyptus treatments clear and rejuvenate" #Your hashtags
CTA	"Revitalize your breath. Book a eucalyptus steam therapy now."

AD 29: SERENE STRESS MELT

Parameter	Description
Title	Serene Stress Melt
Sentiment	Calming
Post Format	Reel
Category	Anxiety Reduction
Language	Gentle and Welcoming
Theme	Serenity
Idea	Focusing on services that help melt away stress and anxiety.
TEXT OVERLAY	"Dissolve Your Stress"
CAPTION	"Let go of your worries in a sanctuary designed for calm" #Your hashtags
CTA	"Find your serenity. Book a stress-melting session today."

AD 30: LUMINOUS SKIN LEAGUE

Parameter	Description
Title	Luminous Skin League
Sentiment	Confident
Post Format	Reel
Category	Skincare
Language	Bold and Inspiring
Theme	Beauty Boost
Idea	Highlighting facial treatments for radiant skin.
TEXT OVERLAY	"Glow with Confidence"
CAPTION	"Dull skin? Join our Luminous Skin League with our signature facials" #Your hashtags
CTA	"Shine bright with radiant skin. Schedule your facial today."

AD 31: DETOXIFY YOUR LIFE

Parameter	Description
Title	Detoxify Your Life
Sentiment	Empowering
Post Format	Reel
Category	Detoxification
Language	Motivating and Supportive
Theme	Cleanse
Idea	Showcasing detox spa treatments that help flush out toxins.
TEXT OVERLAY	"Cleanse Your Body & Mind"
CAPTION	"Ready for a reset? Our detox treatments are the fresh start you need" #Your hashtags
CTA	"Begin your detox journey. Book a treatment today."

AD 32: 5 SIGNS YOU NEED A SPA DAY

Parameter	Description
Sentiment	Awareness
Post Format	Carousel
Category	Wellness Awareness
Language	Informative and Engaging
Theme	Self-Care
Idea	Educating about the benefits of taking a spa day.
CARD 1	"Constant Fatigue: Recharge with a revitalizing body wrap."
CARD 2	"Muscle Soreness: Relax with our therapeutic massages."
CARD 3	"Poor Sleep Quality: Drift away with a sleep-inducing head massage."
CARD 4	"Skin Dullness: Brighten up with our organic facials."
CARD 5	"High Stress Levels: Unwind with aromatherapy sessions."
CAPTION	"Recognize these signs? It's your body calling for a spa day. Swipe to see how we can help" #Your hashtags
CTA	"Don't ignore the signs. Book your spa experience

AD 33: JOURNEY TO RELAXATION

Parameter	Description
Sentiment	Tranquility
Post Format	Carousel
Category	Spa Services
Language	Calming and Soothing
Theme	Relaxation Journey
Idea	Showcasing a step-by-step relaxation experience at the spa.
CARD 1	"Welcome Ritual: Begin with a warm tea and calming ambiance."
CARD 2	"Hydrotherapy: Soak in our mineral-rich waters for balance."
CARD 3	"Custom Massage: Select your preferred massage techniques and oils."
CARD 4	"Post-Spa Glow: Leave feeling refreshed and radiant."
CAPTION	"Embark on a journey to peace and calm. Swipe to see how our spa can transform your day" #Your hashtags
CTA	"Ready for tranquility? Start your journey with us today."

AD 34: BEAT THE WORK STRESS

Parameter	Description
Sentiment	Encouraging
Post Format	Carousel
Category	Stress Management
Language	Supportive and Understanding
Theme	Workplace Wellness
Idea	Offering solutions for work-related stress.
CARD 1	"Tension Headaches: Relieve them with our head and neck massages."
CARD 2	"Stiff Shoulders: Ease them with hot stone therapy."
CARD 3	"Eye Strain: Rest them with our soothing eye treatments."
CARD 4	"Mental Fatigue: Rejuvenate with our signature aromatherapy."
CARD 5	"Lack of Focus: Restore it with our mindfulness meditation sessions."
CAPTION	"Work stress can take a toll. Swipe to see how our spa services can help you reset" #Your hashtags
CTA	"Take the step to de-stress. Book your escape today."

AD 35: HYDRATION HEAVEN

Parameter	Description
Title	Hydration Heaven
Sentiment	Rejuvenating
Post Format	Carousel
Category	Skin Hydration
Language	Fresh and Uplifting
Theme	Moisturizing Mastery
CARD 1	"Splash into Hydration" (Image: Refreshing facial mist)
CARD 2	"Deep Dive for Your Skin" (Image: Hydrating mask application)
CARD 3	"Nutrition for a Luminous Look" (Image: Nutrient-rich serums)
CARD 4	"Lock in the Moisture" (Image: Finalizing treatment with a rich cream)
CAPTION	"Quench your skin's thirst with our moisture infusing treatments" #Your hashtags
CTA	"Drench your skin in hydration. Book your session today."

AD 36: BACK PAIN BE GONE

Parameter	Description
Title	Back Pain Be Gone
Sentiment	Relief
Post Format	Carousel
Category	Pain Management
Language	Comforting and Assuring
Theme	Back Pain Solutions
CARD 1	"Identify the Tension" (Image: Therapist assessing a client's back)
CARD 2	"Targeted Treatments" (Image: Specialized back massage)
CARD 3	"Sustain the Comfort" (Image: Client learning stretch exercises)
CAPTION	"Turn your back on pain with our targeted back treatments" #Your hashtags
CTA	"Bid farewell to back pain. Schedule your appointment now."

AD 37: AGE GRACEFULLY

Parameter	Description
Title	Age Gracefully
Sentiment	Empowering
Post Format	Carousel
Category	Anti-Aging
Language	Positive and Reassuring
Theme	Timeless Beauty
CARD 1	"Nature's Timekeepers" (Image: Antioxidant-rich treatments)
CARD 2	"Gentle Yet Effective" (Image: Non-invasive skin tightening)
CARD 3	"Hydration at Every Age" (Image: Moisturizing regimens)
CARD 4	"Reflect Your Experience" (Image: Happy, older client looking rejuvenated)
CAPTION	"Age is just a number, but your skin doesn't have to count them" #Your hashtags
CTA	"Embrace your age with grace. Book our anti-aging treatments today."

AD 38: THE ANTI-STRESS TOOLKIT

Parameter	Description
Title	The Anti-Stress Toolkit
Sentiment	Empowering
Post Format	Carousel
Category	Stress Management
Language	Reassuring and Helpful
Theme	Stress-Free Living
Idea	Sharing a series of spa services and tips to combat stress.
Card 1	Understanding stress and its impact on health.
Card 2	Relaxing massages that target stress relief.
Card 3	Soothing sound baths and their calming effect.
Card 4	Exclusive deal for a complete anti-stress package.
TEXT OVERLAY	"Your Path to Peace Begins Here"
CAPTION	"Overwhelmed by stress? Swipe for our ultimate stress-busting services" #Your hashtags
CTA	"Unwind the day—book your anti-stress treatment now."

AD 39: GLOWING MATERNITY MOMENTS

Parameter	Description
Title	Glowing Maternity Moments
Sentiment	Joyful
Post Format	Carousel
Category	Prenatal Care
Language	Warm and Nurturing
Theme	Maternity Wellness
Idea	Highlighting spa treatments that are safe and beneficial for pregnancy.
Card 1	The importance of self-care during pregnancy.
Card 2	Prenatal massage benefits for mother and baby.
Card 3	Gentle yoga classes for expectant mothers.
Card 4	Safe skincare products and treatments for pregnancy.
TEXT OVERLAY	"Celebrate Your Pregnancy with Pampering"
CAPTION	"Expecting moms deserve the best care. Swipe to see how we cater to you" #Your hashtags
CTA	"Book your maternity spa day."

AD 40: DETOX DYNAMICS

Parameter	Description
Title	Detox Dynamics
Sentiment	Cleansing
Post Format	Carousel
Category	Body Detox
Language	Clear and Invigorating
Theme	Detox Journey
Idea	Exploring the benefits of detoxifying spa treatments.
Card 1	Why your body needs a detox and what it means.
Card 2	Detoxifying therapies: Body wraps and scrubs.
Card 3	Nutritional advice for supporting a detox.
Card 4	How to maintain detox results with daily routines.
TEXT OVERLAY	"Refresh Your System, Renew Your Spirit"
CAPTION	"Ready for a reset? Our detox treatments offer a fresh start" #Your hashtags
CTA	"Embark on your detox adventure. Sign up today."

AD 41: QUICK STRESS-BUSTER MASSAGE TECHNIQUES

Parameter	Description
Title	Quick Stress-Buster Massage Techniques
Sentiment	Relaxing, Educational
Post Format	Reel
Category	Massage Services
Language	Simple, Direct, Soothing
Theme	Quick Relaxation
Idea	Showcase short clips of massage techniques that alleviate stress quickly.
Video	Therapist demonstrating techniques on a client with calming music.
Text Overlay	"5-minute stress relief"
Caption	"Stressful day? Unwind with our quick massage techniques that fit into your lunch break!" #Your hashtags
CTA	"Swipe up to book your quick escape!"

AD 42: HYDRATION HEAVEN WATER-BASED SPA TREATMENTS

Parameter	Description
Title	Hydration Heaven
Sentiment	Refreshing, Invigorating
Post Format	Story
Category	Hydration Treatments
Language	Engaging, Inviting
Theme	Skin Hydration
Idea	Highlight the importance of skin hydration and showcase your water-based treatments.
Image	A serene image of a hydration facial mask being applied.
Text Overlay	"Dive into Hydration"
Caption	"Keep your skin quenched with our hydration treatments!" #Your hashtags
CTA	"Tap to book your hydration treatment!"

AD 43: AROMATIC BLISS - ESSENTIAL OIL COLLECTION

Parameter	Description
Title	Aromatic Bliss
Sentiment	Soothing, Luxurious
Post Format	Single Image
Category	Aromatherapy
Language	Rich, Descriptive
Theme	Aromatherapy Benefits
Idea	Showcase the range of essential oils used in spa treatments.
Image	A collection of essential oil bottles with a serene spa background.
Text Overlay	"Scents of Serenity"
Caption	"Elevate your senses with our curated essential oils" #Your hashtags
CTA	"Discover your scent. Visit us today."

AD 44: THE ULTIMATE RELAXATION PACKAGE

Parameter	Description
Title	The Ultimate Relaxation Package
Sentiment	Luxurious, Relaxing
Post Format	Carousel
Category	Spa Packages
Language	Elegant, Soothing
Theme	Complete Relaxation
Idea	Introduce a spa package that includes various relaxing treatments.
Card 1	Introduction to the relaxation package.
Card 2	Benefits of the full-body massage included.
Card 3	Features of the aromatherapy session.
Card 4	Glimpse of the tranquil environment.
Text Overlay	"Your relaxation journey starts here"
Caption	"Indulge in the ultimate relaxation experience with our special package" #Your hashtags
CTA	"Book your journey to tranquility."

AD 45: DETOX DELIGHT

Parameter	Description
Title	Detox Delight
Sentiment	Energizing, Cleansing
Post Format	Reel
Category	Detox & Wellness
Language	Inspirational, Informative
Theme	Detoxification
Idea	Showcase a day of detox with healthy juices and spa treatments that support cleansing.
Video	A vibrant display of juices followed by detoxifying spa treatments.
Text Overlay	"Cleanse & Rejuvenate"
Caption	"Detox your body, refresh your mind with our Detox Delight package" #Your hashtags
CTA	"Start your detox journey; book now!"

AD 46: DEEP SLEEP INDUCING MASSAGE TECHNIQUES

Parameter	Description
Title	Deep Sleep Inducing Massage Techniques
Sentiment	Relaxing, Peaceful
Post Format	Reel
Category	Sleep Enhancement
Language	Calming, Soft
Theme	Sleep Improvement
Idea	Demonstrating massage techniques that promote better sleep
Video	Clips of a therapist performing gentle massages
Text Overlay	"Slip into a Deep Sleep"
Caption	"Discover our massage techniques for a night of deep, restful sleep. Say goodbye to restless nights!" #Your hashtags
CTA	"Book your sleep-enhancing massage today!"

AD 47: HERBAL STEAM THERAPY - DETOXIFY YOUR BODY

Parameter	Description
Title	Herbal Steam Therapy
Sentiment	Cleansing, Invigorating
Post Format	Story
Category	Detoxification
Language	Informative, Refreshing
Theme	Body Cleansing
Idea	Showcasing the benefits of herbal steam therapy
Image	A serene image of the steam therapy room
Text Overlay	"Detoxify with Herbal Steam"
Caption	"Embrace the purifying power of our Herbal Steam Therapy. A natural way to cleanse your body and mind" #Your hashtags
CTA	"Tap to book your detox session!"

AD 48: REVITALIZE WITH OUR SIGNATURE FACIALS

Parameter	Description
Title	Revitalize with Our Signature Facials
Sentiment	Refreshing, Beautifying
Post Format	Single Image
Category	Skin Care
Language	Elegant, Descriptive
Theme	Facial Treatments
Idea	Highlighting the unique benefits of the spa's facials
Image	Close-up of a soothing facial treatment
Text Overlay	"Revitalize Your Skin"
Caption	"Transform your skin with our signature facials. Experience rejuvenation and a radiant glow" #Your hashtags
CTA	"Book your facial rejuvenation today!"

AD 49: ULTIMATE HYDRATION THERAPY

Parameter	Description
Title	Ultimate Hydration Therapy
Sentiment	Nourishing, Refreshing
Post Format	Story
Category	Skin Hydration
Language	Visual, Descriptive
Theme	Deep Skin Hydration
Idea	Promoting a hydration therapy for radiant skin
Image	A glowing, hydrated skin after treatment
Text Overlay	"Quench Your Skin's Thirst"
Caption	"Dive into deep hydration with our Ultimate Hydration Therapy. Perfect for restoring moisture and achieving that healthy glow!" #Your hashtags
CTA	"Swipe up to achieve your skin's best glow!"

AD 50: GARDEN SERENITY

Parameter	Description
Title	Garden Serenity
Sentiment	Peaceful
Post Format	Reels
Category	Themed Promotion
Language	Short Caption
Theme	Garden
Idea	A quick reel featuring garden-inspired relaxation techniques
Reel	Lush garden visual with meditation spots
Text Overlay	"Find Peace In Our Garden Spa"
Caption	" Let nature's serenity bloom around you!" #Your hashtags
CTA	" Cultivate calmness! Reserve your garden spa experience today!"

ABOUT THE AUTHOR

Argenis Soutelo is Ph.D in Education. Strategist in Digital Marketing, Digital Trafficker, Content Producer, Certificate in Marketing by UCLA, University of California, Los Angeles, and Google in Digital Marketing and E-commerce, Digital Analytics and Google Ads. Media Buying Professional by Meta. He has successfully grown his social media presence from 0 to 82 000 followers on Facebook, Instagram, YouTube, and outstanding results in Google Search which improved the enrollments in his school business 17%. He has invested more than $ 100 000 in ads for his customers with remarkable success. He developed skills in team leadership and time management. He also created an online English course with all the strategy campaigns, seed launch, email marketing, and automatizations to launch the product. He has worked with digital campaigns to strengthen brand awareness, consideration, and conversion for different digital products.

We Value Your Feedback!

As we reach the final page of "50 Instagram and Facebook Ads: A Practical Guide 2024", I hope that you found the insights and strategies within these pages both enlightening and practical. Your journey towards mastering digital marketing does not end here, and I believe your insights can greatly benefit others embarking on a similar path.

Could We Ask for a Moment of Your Time?

Your thoughts and experiences are incredibly valuable, not just to me, but to fellow readers and aspiring digital marketers. If you could take a moment to leave a review on Amazon KDP, it would be immensely appreciated. Your review can help bring this book to more readers, offering them the guidance they need to excel in their social media marketing endeavors.

Leaving a Review is Easy:

1. Go to the Amazon page where you purchased the book.
2. Scroll down to the 'Customer Reviews' section.
3. Click 'Write a customer review'.
4. Share your thoughts, experiences, and how the book helped you.

Every review counts, and your support is instrumental in helping me reach and assist more people in achieving their digital marketing goals. Thank you for your time, your purchase, and your invaluable contribution to the community of digital marketers.

Warm regards,

A.V. SOUTELO